Concert and Contest COLLECTION

T0071595

Compiled and Edited by H. VOXMAN

for

Bb TENOR SAXOPHONE

CONTENTS

RUBANK ®

HAL•LEONARD ®
CORPORATION
7777 W. BLUEMOUND RD. P.O. BOX 13819 MILWAUKEE, WI 53213

COLLECTIONS IN THIS SERIES:

C Flute and Piano

Bb Clarinet and Piano

Bb Bass Clarinet and Piano

Oboe and Piano

Bassoon and Piano

Eb Alto Saxophone and Piano

Bb Tenor Saxophone and Piano

Bb Cornet, Trumpet
or Baritone and Piano
(Baritone In Bass or Treble Clef)

French Horn (In F) and Piano

Trombone (Bass Clef) and Piano

Eb or BBb Bass
(Tuba - Sousaphone) and Piano

Viola and Piano

Individually Compiled and Edited, Each Of the Collections Includes A Diversified Repertoire
The Solo Parts and Piano Accompaniments Are Published As Separate Books With A Durable Cover

Contradance

Bb Tenor Saxophone

W. A. MOZART
Transcribed by H. Voxman

Sinfonia
(Arioso)
from Cantata No. 156*

Bb Tenor Saxophone

J. S. BACH
Transcribed by H. Voxman

---

* This Cantata was composed by Bach ca. 1730. The original scoring of the Sinfonia is for solo oboe, strings, and continuo. The eighth-note accompaniment figures (treble) should probably be played quasi pizzicato. Bach also used this melody in a more elaborate version in his F minor Concerto for Clavier.

Allegretto

Bb Tenor Saxophone

A. ARENSKY
Transcribed by H. Voxman

Valse Nouvelle
from Album for the Young

Bb Tenor Saxophone

P. TCHAIKOVSKY, Op. 39, No. 8
Transcribed by H. Voxman

Menuetto and Presto
from Trio V

Bb Tenor Saxophone

F. J. HAYDN
Transcribed by H. Voxman

Two Little Tales

Bb Tenor Saxophone

E. DESPORTES
Transcribed by H. Voxman

I - SENTIMENTAL

II - GAY

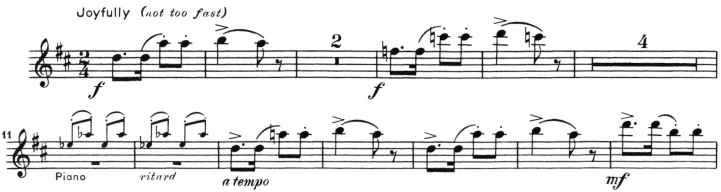

The Old Castle
from Pictures at an Exhibition

Bb Tenor Saxophone

M. MUSSORGSKY
Transcribed by H. Voxman

Pièce in G Minor

Bb Tenor Saxophone

GABRIEL PIERNÉ, Op. 5
Transcribed by H. Voxman

Première Étude de Concours

Bb Tenor Saxophone

A. S. PETIT
Edited by H. Voxman

Prelude and Allegro

Bb Tenor Saxophone

LEROY OSTRANSKY

Novelette

Bb Tenor Saxophone

GEORGES SPORCK
Edited by H. Voxman

First Concertino

Bb Tenor Saxophone

GEORGES GUILHAUD
Transcribed by H. Voxman

Adagio and Allegro
(from Sonata No. 6 for Violin & Keyboard)

Bb Tenor Saxophone

G. F. HANDEL
Transcribed by H. Voxman

Gigue
from Partita III for Solo Violin

Bb Tenor Saxophone
(Unaccompanied)

J. S. BACH
Transcribed by H. Voxman

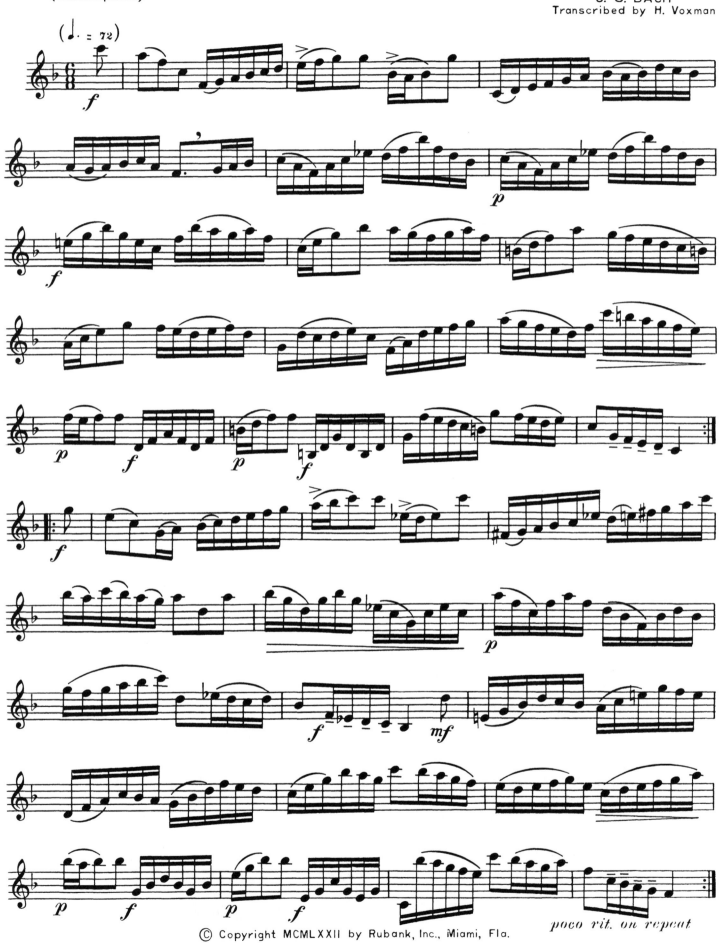

poco rit. on repeat